the misfits

To calm herself down, Susan petted her bunny gently but firmly.

Tired of forgetting the time, Snodgrass finally has a watch surgically embedded into his wrist.

As a last resort,
Etch A Sketch Chaz
advertises his longing
to the world.

Frustrated with her "anger management" workshops, Paula finally builds a chimney out of her forehead.

Everyone – especially the children – dreaded "Crazy Dave," the finger puppet man.

As startling testament
to the old adage
"you are what you eat",
Hobely Pobbleton, a
run-o-the-mill
homebody, has nearly
transformed into a
trembling blob of
jello.

Tunny hopes a
toilet plunger
will do some
good.

Explaining the gesture as "a shortcut to illumination," Erasmus bursts forth in his self-fashioned lightning-rod hat.

Eugene is an usher
by vocation, but he
dreams of someday
becoming a superstar.

Martha Rosenbaum
one of Hollywood's
most menacing
celebrity chasers.

Suddenly,
he felt happy.
He did not know why.
He tried to capture the
feeling in a net.

Some men, like
Steig, will stop
at nothing to
establish a sense
of identity.

Walter carries a
Watermelon of
Sorrow.

Clyde Battle,
corporate walrus,
lumbers down another
synthetic hallway.

In a desperate
attempt to
introduce some
spirituality into her
life, Veronica has
sculpted her hair
into a cathedral.

Tippy the chinless policeman fancies himself something of a dandy.

In his dreams, Pinwheel Joey drifts above all the houses and streets in his neighborhood.

Though spurned by most intellectual circles, Inez still makes an occasional appearance at the gallery openings.

As a last resort, Armand sends his self-fashioned peri-glasses up above the troubled waters of his life.

He had forgotten that he
was a mime and that
his box was imaginary.
He just wanted to
get out and live
like an ordinary
person.

Even her
Tootsi Plohound
platforms fail
to offset
Ingeborg's
hopelessly brainy
appearance.

Refusing to be pigeonholed as an effete intellectual, Glenn ventures out to the courts.

Desperate for some
form of rejuvenation,
Lambert has installed
an electrical socket
in his forehead.

Fresh from the ward, Chatterton embarks on his new career.

One-legged Tracy, with pet bird McGaffeney, anxiously waves good-bye to parents before she hops off to college.

Sabrina wasn't "talking to herself." She was just addressing the tiny conductor on top of her head.

Mile-o-minute Mitchy explains how he hopes his new poodle-do will save his act from going to the dogs!!!

"It might not be my heart," Nathaniel said. "It's just a goldfish. But it'll keep growing as long as we give it space and time."

Having stumbled upon a dreaded clambake, Umberto's social skills have utterly abandoned him.

Upon the departure of her beloved, through countless nights of weal and woe, Cassandra has at last succeeded at crying her eyes out.

Lionel hopes his lightning-staff shtick will jumpstart his sagging sales.

After the whole Pinocchio fiasco, Geppetto didn't fare much better as a cupcake confectioner.

Amoeba could be
anything to anyone—
which was charming,
of course, but also
rather disturbing.

Henrietta - half-human, half-aardvark - whoops it up at the Valentine's Day ball.

Lego Thom
walls out
the world.

At age 37, Tybald has yet to express, let alone satisfy, his deepest and most painful yearnings.

Ostracized by her
classmates, Georgianna,
half-girl, half-giraffe,
pines for a distant,
kinder star.

Having grown weary of the humdrum day-to-day, Flannery wildly entertains her new ideas.

Never to be truly loved
by either fish or man,
Jordan the hapless
squid-boy ponders his
quasi-aquatic fate.

Lanza the futon salesman prefers not to be bothered by anyone, at any time, under any conditions whatsoever.

Forsythe the
atrophied scholar
and pet bunny,
Panama.

In a gesture of evolutionary defiance, Marshall, age 36, has his diapers custom tailored.

Johannes tends
his secret
garden.

Inveterate Hollywood agent, hobnobber, and bullshit artist Jerry Ball has at last lost control of his own lips.

Dr. Pretzels,
the cross-eyed
psychiatrist

He loved her
So much he
turned yellow,
and his heart,
like a flying fish,
lurched out of
his mouth.

"Thank you for the interest. But we won't be able to offer you the position until you find some means of keeping the birds in your head."

Though in fact
little traveled,
Penelope Poptart,
professional envelope
licker, fancies herself
eminently worldly.

Teachers called Jerome a "space cadet." But you'd be one too if invisible rocket ships were using your head as a landing pad.

An evolutionary marvel,
Sheepdog Shostakovitch
has graduated to
the position of
valet-parking
attendant.

The stilts
had helped boost
Henry's self-esteem
for a little while,
but he knew he
was heading for
a fall.

Marvin was the kind of man who always needed to measure and weigh everything: in short, he was a burden and an annoyance to everyone.

Overwhelmed by the
passage of time,
Nicholson cried tiny
clocks.

"Dumpling," his grandmother called him, and the name stuck, and everybody hated him.

Elwin was the sort
of kid who ate
tongue sandwiches-
silent, withdrawn, and
prone to morbid
contemplation.

When Max's face
transformed into
a manhole cover,
his friends called
it an "inevitable
manifestation of
the aching abyss
within him."

Tired of attempting to
"control his life,"
Heironymous casts his
fate to the winds.

Jasper had little
to offer but the
products of his
jumbled and riotous
mind.

When it comes to "Working a room," no one can match Mistress Pythagoras

Samuel was "wonderful," "sweet," "kind," "funny," "intelligent," "generous," "polite," and single.

No one seems
particularly
interested in
Gregorian's Paper
bells.

A Note on the Author

Jon Rosen has been a cabdriver, a temp, a security guard, a television show transcriber, a foot messenger, a personal assistant, a theater house manager, a professional "namer," and a gardener at an Episcopal seminary. He is currently launching the Misfits Greeting Card Company in Great Barrington, Massachusetts, where he lives with his wife and son.